AN ORANGE
Poetry
PAINTBOX

CHOSEN BY JOHN FOSTER

OXFORD
UNIVERSITY PRESS

Oxford University Press, Great Clarendon Street, Oxford OX2 6DP

Oxford   New York
Athens   Auckland   Bangkok   Bogotá   Buenos Aires
Calcutta   Cape Town   Chennai   Dar es Salaam
Delhi   Florence   Hong Kong   Istanbul   Karachi
Kuala Lumpur   Madrid   Melbourne   Mexico City
Mumbai   Nairobi   Paris   São Paulo   Shanghai
Singapore Taipei   Tokyo   Toronto   Warsaw

and associated companies in
Berlin   Ibadan

First published in paperback 1996
Reissued in this edition 2001

A CIP catalogue record for this book is available from the British Library

Illustrations by

Jane Bottomley, Diana Catchpole, Andy Cooke, Paul Dowling,
Jackie East, Jane Gedye, Frank James, Jolyne Knox, Angela Denise Lindsay,
Lynda Murray, Rachael O'Neill, Claire Pound, Amelia Rosato, Graham Round,
Samantha Rugen, Lisa Smith, Kay Widdowson, Merida Woodford

ISBN 0 19 919420 3

Printed in Hong Kong

Contents

Carnival time

Sing me a song.
Tell me a rhyme.
Dance me a dance.
It's carnival time.

Put on a costume.
Paint your face.
Beat those drums
all over the place.

Sing me a song.
Tell me a rhyme.
Dance me a dance.
It's carnival time.

Tony Mitton

Camping out

One night last holiday
We camped on our lawn.
We planned to stay out there
From darkness to dawn.

But at half-past ten
When the garden was black,
We rushed into the house
Shouting, 'Mum, we've come back.'

Clive Webster

On holiday with Grandma

When we took Grandma to the beach
she dug a deep hole in the wet sand,
knocked down my row of castles,
caught red crabs in the rock pools,
went in the sea right up to her knees,
walked in some clay
so it squished through her toes,
tied long, green seaweed in her hair,
played cricket, had an ice-cream,
and threw a bucket of water over Dad.
Grandma said she had not had so
much fun for years.

Robin Mellor

Postcard

I didn't want to come to Spain,
but now I'm really glad I came.

The weather here is always fine.
Skies are blue here all the time.

I love the sand, the sea and sun.
I'm having lots and lots of fun.

Yesterday I had the chance
to learn to do a Spanish dance.

I'm learning to speak Spanish too.
'Como está' means 'How are you'.

I didn't want to come to Spain,
but now I hope I'll come again!

Adios!

Tony Langham

Seaside in winter

Most people like the seaside
In summer when it's warm,
But I would rather be there
During a winter storm.

The beach is quite deserted,
Only the great waves roar,
And seagulls drift like paper birds
Above the windswept shore.

Daphne Lister

Out-time, in-time

Out-time, out-time,
run around and shout time,
shake it all about time,
out-time, out-time.

In-time, in-time,
it's time to begin time,
stop the noisy din time,
in-time, in-time.

Brian Moses

Tiger tag

Tiger tag! Tiger tag!
One, two, three!
Tiger tag! Tiger tag!
You can't catch me!

Harry got an elephant
just for a pet.
Harry took it home
in a jumbo jet.

Larry got a lion
and took it to the zoo.
Kerry got a tiger
and I've got YOU!

Tony Mitton

Playground problems

Please, Miss:
Kevin Jones has
burst his blister;
And Charlotte says
that Robert kissed her:
He says he tried to
but he missed her.
And Miss, they're swinging
on the trees,
And Trevor Tonks
has cut his knees,
And Amy's found
a bunch of keys . . .

It's urgent!
Can you come, Miss, please?

Eric Finney

19

Conkers

This is a beauty,
brown and shiny.
The other conkers
all look tiny.

I thread the string
and then take aim.
I know I'm bound
to win the game.

I've had my go
and scored a hit.
Now Jenny tries
and misses it.

Another go.
I'm doing well.
Then Jenny's turn.
You just can't tell

Who's going to win.
She takes a hit.
Oh no! She's won!
My conker's split!

Jill Townsend

Inside, outside

When I'm sitting in class
I can't wait to get out,
To run and to chase
And to scramble about.

When I'm out in the cold
And the shivers begin
And the wind and the rain—
I can't wait to get in.

Richard James

23

The roller coaster

I rode the roller coaster.
It gave me such a scare.
I thought I'd left my tummy
floating in the air.

Marian Swinger

One summer evening

We were playing cricket
in the garden after school.
Dad dived for a catch,
but he missed
and fell in the paddling pool!

John Foster

Hibernating hedgehog

Here comes winter,
cold and grey.
The hedgehog tucks
itself away.

Here comes ice
and here comes snow.
It needs somewhere
warm to go.

Here comes mist
and freezing fog.
Here's a good old
hollow log.

And here's a pile
of leaves that's deep.
It rolls up tight
and goes to sleep.

Tony Mitton

Seasons of trees

In spring
The trees
Are a beautiful sight
Dressed in blossom
Pink and white.

In summer
The trees
Are full of treats
Apples and pears
And cherries to eat.

In autumn
The trees
Are red and gold
And the leaves fall down
As the days grow cold.

In winter
The trees
Are bare and plain
Waiting for spring
To dress them again.

Julie Holder

29

Winter walk

Walking home from Granny's
On a dark and snowy night,
Everything looks ghostly
In the shadowy street light.

All is still and quiet.
No footsteps can be heard,
Except the crunch beneath us.
Too cold to say a word.

Wendy Larmont

Footprints

In the winter
watch me go,
making footprints
in the snow.

In the spring
my boots are wet.
See how deep
the puddles get.

In the summer
by the sea,
sandy footprints
made by me.

In the autumn
trees are brown.
I kick the leaves
all over town!

Irene Rawnsley

Harvest time

Harvest time! Harvest time!
It's harvest time again.
Time to cut the corn
And gather in the grain.

Harvest time! Harvest time!
Time to pick the fruits,
To gather in the nuts
And dig up all the roots.

Harvest time! Harvest time!
In the autumn sun
We'll cut, pick and dig
Until the harvest's done.

John Foster

Catch them if you can!

Chickens and hens,
chickens and hens!
Chicks in the farmyard
chicks in the pens,
chicks in the kitchen,
under the chairs,
chicks on the doorstep,
chicks on the stairs . . .

Chickens and hens,
chickens and hens,
chicks in the farmyard
but NONE in the pens!

Judith Nicholls

The cow in the storm

The sky turned grey,
The horse went 'Neigh',
But the cow just went on chewing.

The sky turned black,
The ducks went 'Quack',
But the cow just went on chewing.

Lightning sparked,
The farm dogs barked,
But the cow just went on chewing.

Raindrops splashed,
The farm cats dashed,
But the cow just went on chewing.

Showers stopped,
Rabbits hopped,
But the cow just went on chewing.

Sunshine streamed,
The whole farm steamed,
But the cow,
The cow,
The cow,
The cow,
But the cow just went on chewing.

Richard Edwards

I'd like to be a farmer

I'd like to be a farmer
With animals to feed,
And a tractor to drive along
When I am sowing seed.

I'd like to be a farmer.
I'd walk in muddy boots
And watch the brown fields
   turning green
With tender, growing shoots.

I'd like to be a farmer.
After months of sun and rain
I'd drive a combine harvester
To cut the golden grain.

Eric Finney

The barn owl

High up on the rafters
Something white
Sleeps in the shadows
Waiting for the night.

High up from the rafters
Something flies,
With silent wings
And big round eyes.

Richard James

44

Chicks

Yesterday
They were warm, brown eggs.
Now they're fluffy, yellow balls
On legs.

Eric Finney

The tractor

The tractor is rough and ready
To do whatever it can.
It snorts and it chuffs and it roars
And its wheels
Are as tall as a man.
It clears the fields
Of rocks and stumps.
It takes the rubbish
To tips and dumps.

It ploughs the furrows
To plant the seed.
It takes the feed
To sheep in snow.
Wherever you want
It will try to go.
The tractor is rough and ready
To do whatever it can.
It snorts and it chuffs and it roars
And its wheels
Are as tall as a man.

Julie Holder

Wrong trolley

Mum, there's catfood in our trolley
And we haven't got a cat!
There's a big bag of potatoes
And we didn't load up that.
Do you remember loading beans
Or peas or cauliflowers?
Mum, I know we're pushing it
But is this trolley ours?

Eric Finney

Play shop

With plastic pounds and pennies
and play-dough cakes and sweets,
it's not the sort of shop
you'd find in real streets.

Sweet

In between the play house
and the sand and water tray,
this shop is in the classroom
where the shoppers only play.

Celia Warren

shop

51

The corner shop

It sells apples, green and red,
It sells poppadoms and bread,
It sells comics, it sells coffee,
It sells envelopes and toffee,
It sells carrots, it sells cheese,
It sells stamps and frozen peas,
It sells noodles, it sells string,
It sells every single thing.

Richard James

Whoops!

Our supermarket keeps baked beans
inside a plastic bin.
They used to pile them on the floor
till James picked up the BOTTOM tin!

Judith Nicholls

Night fright

My hair stood on end
and I trembled with fright
when I heard a strange noise
on the stairs in the night.

'CREAK', it went.
'EEK', I went.
What should I do?
Then my brother
leaped into my room
and yelled, 'BOO!'

Marian Swinger

Mixed feelings

I stayed at my friend's
And that made me glad.
I wanted to play
With a toy that she had;
She said that I couldn't
And that made me mad.

I shouted at her
That made me feel bad.
And now we're not friends
And that makes me feel sad.

Julie Holder

Bertie the hamster

Every Sunday I clean Bertie's cage.
I tip his bedding into the bin,
I give his food to the birds,
I pour his water down the sink.

But today there is no Bertie to put back.
Dad says that he had a good life
and two is very old for a hamster.
I look into his empty cage
And remember his soft nose,
His warm fur,
And his tiny body sitting on my hand.

John Coldwell

My new brother

We used to be three—
Mum, Dad and me.
But now there's another.
My new baby brother.

He cries in the night
And sleeps in the day.
He hasn't any idea
Of how to play.

My baby brother's name is Joe.
I just can't wait for him to grow.

Eric Finney and John Foster

Birthday surprises

When I see my presents
on my birthday
I feel excited.
I wonder what surprises are
hiding inside.

When I open my presents
on my birthday
I feel delighted
as I see the surprises
hiding inside.

John Foster

Index of first lines

Acknowledgements

The Editor and Publisher are grateful for permission to include the following poems:

John Coldwell for 'Bertie the hamster' © 1996 John Coldwell; Richard Edwards for 'The cow in the storm' © 1996 Richard Edwards; Eric Finney for 'Chicks', 'I'd like to be a farmer', 'Playground problems' and 'Wrong trolley' all © 1996 Eric Finney; Eric Finney and John Foster for 'My new brother' © 1996 Eric Finney and John Foster; John Foster for 'Birthday surprises', 'Harvest time' and 'One summer evening' all © 1996 John Foster; Julie Holder for 'Mixed feelings', 'Seasons of trees' and 'The tractor' all © 1996 Julie Holder; Richard James for 'Inside, outside', 'The barn owl' and 'The corner shop' all © 1996 Richard James; Tony Langham for 'Postcard' © 1996 Tony Langham; Wendy Larmont for 'Winter walk' © 1996 Wendy Larmont; Daphne Lister for 'Seaside in winter' © 1996 Daphne Lister; Robin Mellor for 'On holiday with Grandma' © 1996 Robin Mellor; Tony Mitton for 'Carnival time', 'Hibernating hedgehog' and 'Tiger tag' all © 1996 Tony Mitton; Brian Moses for 'Out-time, in-time' © 1996 Brian Moses; Judith Nicholls for 'Catch them if you can!' and 'Whoops!' both © 1996 Judith Nicholls; Irene Rawnsley for 'Footprints' © 1996 Irene Rawnsley; Marian Swinger for 'Night fright' and 'The roller coaster' both © 1996 Marian Swinger; Jill Townsend for 'Conkers' © 1996 Jill Townsend; Celia Warren for 'Play shop' © 1996 Celia Warren; Clive Webster for 'Camping out' © 1996 Clive Webster.

Every effort has been made to contact the owners of copyright material, but if any omissions have been made, owners may contact the Publisher, and correct acknowledgement will be made in future editions.